A BUG'S DAY

A Spider's Day

by Elizabeth Neuenfeldt
Illustrated by Claudia Marianno

BLASTOFF! MISSIONS

BLASTOFF! MISSIONS, AN IMPRINT OF BELLWETHER MEDIA BY FLUTTERBEE

Blastoff! Missions takes you on a learning adventure! Colorful illustrations and exciting narratives highlight cool facts about our world and beyond. Read the mission goals and follow the narrative to gain knowledge, build reading skills, and have fun!

Traditional Nonfiction

Narrative Nonfiction

Blastoff! Universe

MISSION GOALS

- FIND YOUR SIGHT WORDS IN THE BOOK.
- LEARN HOW A SPIDER MAKES ITS WEB.
- LEARN HOW A SPIDER CATCHES FOOD.

This edition first published in 2027 by Bellwether Media, Inc.

For information regarding permission, write to Bellwether Media, Inc., Attention: Permissions Department, 3500 American Blvd W, Suite 150, Bloomington, MN 55431.

Library of Congress Cataloging-in-Publication Data

Names: Neuenfeldt, Elizabeth author | Marianno, Claudia, illustrator. Title: A spider's day / by Elizabeth Neuenfeldt; illustrated by Claudia Marianno.
Description: Minneapolis, Minnesota : Bellwether Media, Inc., 2027. | Series: A bug's day | Includes bibliographical references and index. | Audience: Ages 5-8 | Audience: Grades 2-3 | Summary: "Vibrant illustrations accompany information about spiders. The narrative nonfiction text is intended for students in kindergarten through third grade."-- Provided by publisher.
Identifiers: LCCN 2026001548 (print) | LCCN 2026001549 (ebook) | ISBN 9798898800895 (library binding) | ISBN 9798898802134 (ebook)
Subjects: LCSH: Spiders--Behavior--Juvenile literature | Spiders--Juvenile literature | Insects--Juvenile literature
Classification: LCC QL458.4 .N48 2027 (print) | LCC QL458.4 (ebook)
LC record available at https://lccn.loc.gov/2026001548
LC ebook record available at https://lccn.loc.gov/2026001549

Editor: Betsy Rathburn Designer: Laura Sowers

Printed in the United States of America, North Mankato, MN.

This is **Blastoff Jimmy**! He is here to help you on your mission and share fun facts along the way!

Table of Contents

A New Night

The sun is setting.
Nighttime is coming.

A lone spider begins to move.
It is ready to start its night!

The spider needs to build a web. Where will it build?

That house looks like a good spot. But that tree looks even better!

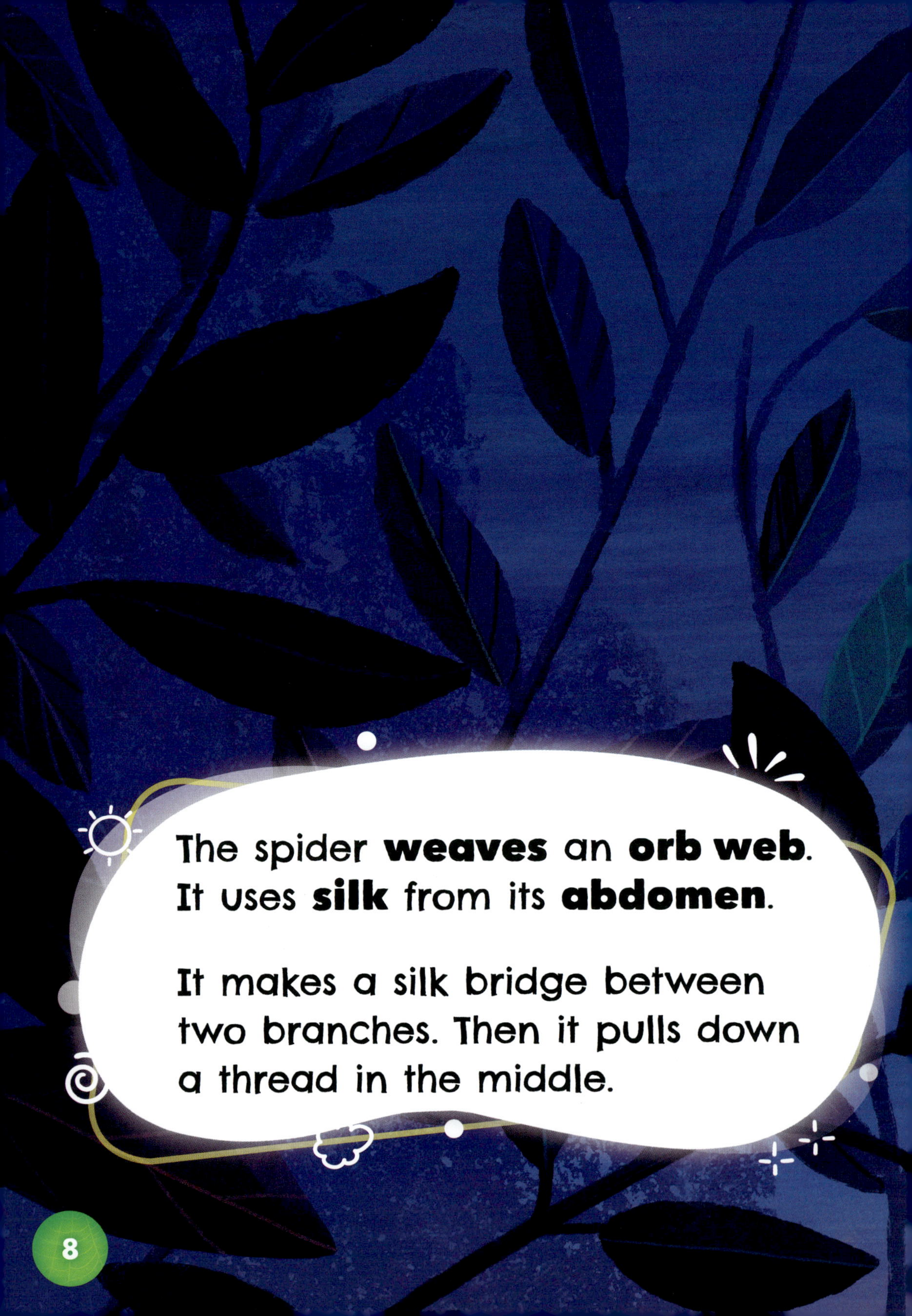

The spider **weaves** an **orb web**. It uses **silk** from its **abdomen**.

It makes a silk bridge between two branches. Then it pulls down a thread in the middle.

abdomen
silk

spokes
orb web

Next, the spider makes silk **spokes** from the center of the web. It makes a zigzag too.

The spider connects the spokes with sticky silk. The orb web is complete!

JIMMY SAYS

Different kinds of spiders make different kinds of webs. Some webs look like sheets. Others are long and thin.

Waiting for Bugs

The spider waits in its web.
Will any **prey** come near?

The spider stays very still.
Its colors help keep birds
and other **predators** away.

Suddenly, a fly gets caught in the web! It gets stuck in the sticky silk.

The spider feels the trapped
bug move the web's spokes.
It knows where the fly is stuck.

The spider creeps toward the fly. The spider bites the bug. The bite spreads **venom**.

The spider uses its legs to wrap the fly in silk. The fly will be a snack later!

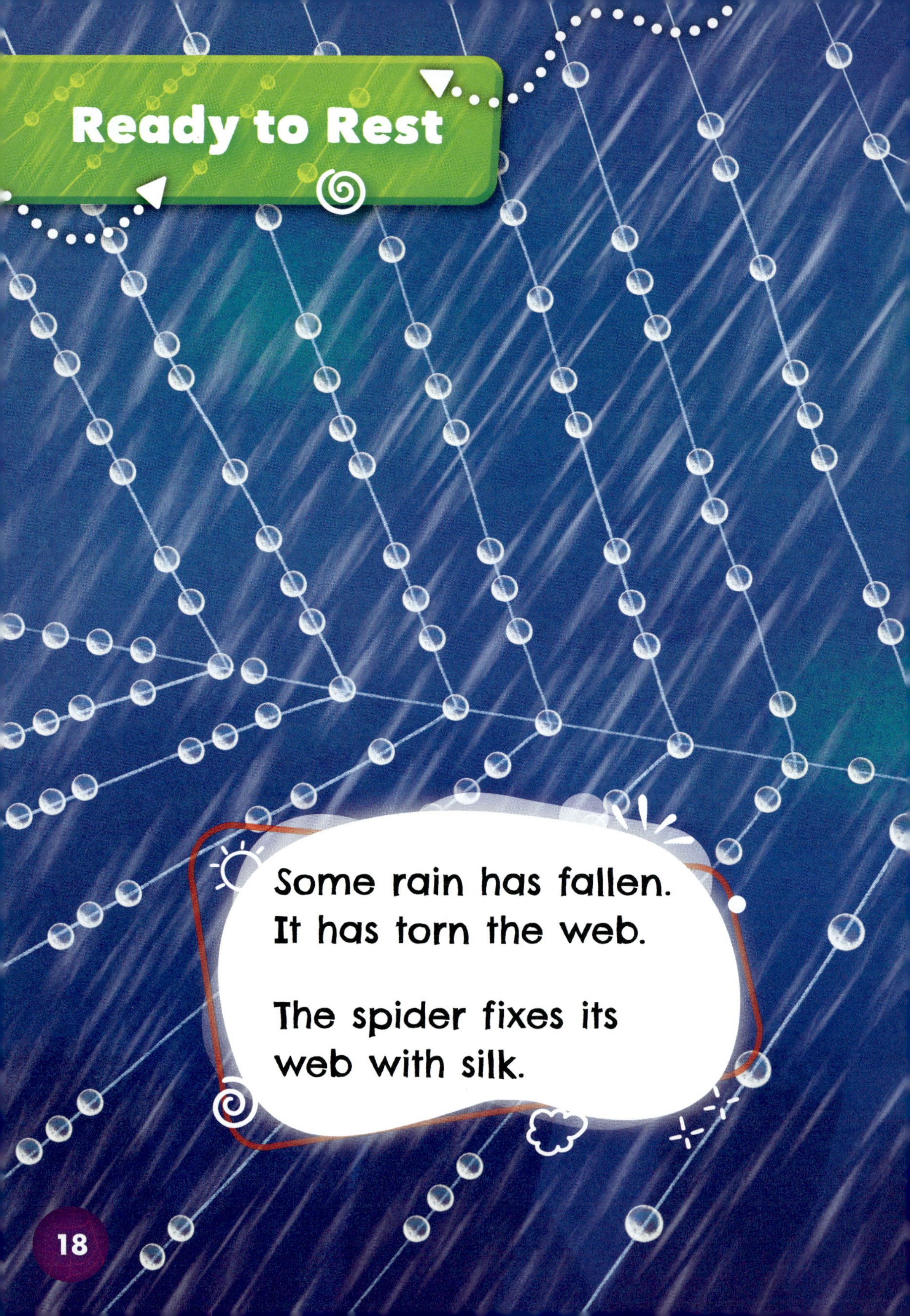

Ready to Rest

Some rain has fallen.
It has torn the web.

The spider fixes its
web with silk.

JIMMY SAYS

Spiders can make up to seven different kinds of silk!

The sun is coming up. It is time for the spider to rest.

It has been a busy night for this web weaver!

All About Spiders

Body Parts

Things Seen

trees

web

fly

Glossary

abdomen–the back part of a spider's body

orb web–a circular, wheel-shaped spider web

predators–animals that hunt other animals for food

prey–animals that are hunted by other animals for food

silk–a thin, strong thread made by spiders

spokes–the small threads coming out from the center of a spider web that help support it

venom–poison produced by an animal, usually for hunting

weaves–forms a web by joining pieces of silk

To Learn More

AT THE LIBRARY

Barth, Kelley. *Biggest and Smallest Spiders.* Parker, Colo.: The Child's World, 2026.

Becker, Becca. *Jumping Spiders.* Minneapolis, Minn.: Jump!, 2025.

Pettiford, Rebecca. *Spiders.* Minneapolis, Minn.: Bellwether Media, 2025.

ON THE WEB

FACTSURFER

Factsurfer.com gives you a safe, fun way to find more information.

1. Go to www.factsurfer.com.

2. Enter "a spider's day" into the search box and click 🔍.

3. Select your book cover to see a list of related content.

BEYOND THE MISSION

> WHAT FACT FROM THE BOOK DID YOU THINK WAS THE MOST INTERESTING?

> DRAW A SPIDER. WHICH BODY PARTS DO YOU THINK ARE THE MOST IMPORTANT?

> DRAW YOUR OWN SPIDER WEB. HOW WOULD YOU MAKE IT STRONG?

Index